Michelle WIE

By Jim Gigliotti

The Child's World
www.childsworld.com

Published in the United States of America by The Child's World®
P.O. Box 326 • Chanhassen, MN 55317-0326
800-599-READ • www.childsworld.com

ACKNOWLEDGMENTS

The Child's World®: Mary Berendes, Publishing Director

Produced by Shoreline Publishing Group LLC
President / Editorial Director: James Buckley, Jr.
Designer: Tom Carling, carlingdesign.com
Cover Art: Slimfilms
Copy Editor: Beth Adelman

Photo Credits
Cover: Getty Images
Interior: AP/Wide World: 5, 8, 12, 19, 20; Corbis: 1; Getty Images: 3, 6,
11, 15, 16, 22, 23, 24, 27, 28

LIBRARY OF CONGRESS
CATALOGING-IN-PUBLICATION DATA

Gigliotti, Jim.
  Michelle Wie / by Jim Gigliotti.
    p. cm. — (The world's greatest athletes)
  Includes bibliographical references and index.
  ISBN 1-59296-757-4 (library bound : alk. paper)
 1. Wie, Michelle—Juvenile literature. 2. Golfers—United States—
Biography—Juvenile literature. 3. Women golfers—United States—
Biography—Juvenile literature. I. Title. II. Series.
  GV964.W49G54 2006
  892.7'16—dc22
                                        2006006293

CONTENTS

Going for the Flagstick!

MICHELLE WIE'S GOLF BALL WAS IN A DIFFICULT position. Her tee shot on the par-3 12th hole had missed the green badly to the left during the second round of the 2005 John Deere Classic.

Now Wie was ankle deep in the rough, with most of her ball hidden in a bed of thick, green grass. She would be lucky if she could get the ball anywhere close to the hole to give herself a chance to save par.

Wie studied her options, pulled out a club, and chipped the ball toward the hole. She wasn't thinking about saving par, though. Instead, she took direct aim at the flagstick. The ball bounced toward the pin and, incredibly, disappeared into the hole for a **birdie**! A mighty roar rose from the crowd of spectators who were following her.

That crowd was following her because Michelle Wie was the only female **amateur** entered in the Professional Golfers Association (PGA) tournament that week—competing against the men.

What's more, though, is that Wie (pronounced "we") was just 15 years old at the time! For a woman golfer to compete against the men is rare. For a teenager, it's unheard of. But it is nothing new for Michelle. The up-and-coming star has been competing against—and beating—boys and girls of all ages since she first picked up a golf club at age 4.

Michelle Wie, shown here at the 2005 John Deere PGA event, has burst onto the world golf scene at a young age.

Michelle demonstrates the picture-perfect swing that has carried her from her youth in Hawaii to golf success.

CHAPTER 1

Swinging for Perfection

IN MANY WAYS, MICHELLE WIE IS A TYPICAL teenager. She calls herself "wacky" and "weird" and says she like to shop more than anything else. A few years ago, she called boys "annoying," but, like most girls her age, she has since changed her mind! She likes going to the movies and hanging out with her pals—when she doesn't have a math test to study for or an essay to write for school. She works hard to earn good grades so she can get into the college she wants (maybe Stanford, she says).

Put a golf club in her hand, though, and Michelle is not a typical teenager at all. In fact, she turns into someone quite **extraordinary**. Her lanky 6-foot frame stands over the ball quietly in a classic posture. Then she coils her body into a swing that unleashes a fury

In Her Own Words

Michelle Wie often has been called a "female Tiger Woods" because both players were outstanding golfers at such an early age. But her long, smooth, and steady swing reminds more people of another notable golfer's—Ernie Els (left), who was the fifth-ranked player in the world entering 2006. Here's Michelle on Ernie Els:

▶ *"My dad really liked Tiger Woods when I started playing golf. He studied Tiger's swing and tried to make my swing like his. But then my swing started to look like Ernie Els'. Now I look at Ernie's swing and I study it and I try to make my swing look like his."*

of power, sometimes sending the ball more than 300 yards down the middle of the fairway. She averages about 290 yards on her drives, and once hit a ball 341 yards. To put that in perspective, the longest hitter on the Ladies Professional Golfers Association (LPGA)

Tour in 2005 was Brittany Lincicome, who averaged 270.3 yards per drive.

Michelle's swing is nearly flawless. It's so perfectly natural, too, that even her coach—the renowned David Leadbetter, who has taught some of the best players in the world—has tinkered very little with it. He wants to let Michelle be herself.

Tom Lehman, a veteran PGA player who has won five tournaments in his career, watched Michelle play a few years ago and gave her the nickname "The Big Wiesy." That's a takeoff on "The Big Easy," which is the nickname for Ernie Els, who is one of the best male golfers in history. Els got his nickname for his long, easy swing. Michelle's swing reminds a lot of people of Ernie's.

Don't let that smooth, easy swing fool you, though. "When you see her hit a golf ball, nothing prepares you for it," PGA star Fred Couples once said. "It's the scariest thing you've ever seen."

That's scary as in good. Unless, of course, you have to play against Michelle. And then you might be a little frightened!

CHAPTER 2

So Young and So Good

DID YOU KNOW THAT WOLFGANG AMADEUS Mozart was only 5 years old when he first began composing his own works of classical music? Or that famous writer Taylor Caldwell wrote her first novel when she was 12? Or that Bobby Fischer was a chess Grandmaster when he was 15?

In sports, Nadia Comaneci was just 14 in 1976 when she won three gold medals and became the first Olympic gymnast to post a perfect score of 10 at the Summer Olympics. Tracy Austin was 14 when she played in the Wimbledon Tennis Championships in England for the first time, also in 1976.

The world has certainly seen young people do amazing things before. The golf world, though, has never seen a young success story quite like Michelle

Michelle's parents are so supportive of her career that her dad B.J. (left) often was her caddy at golf tournaments.

Wie—and that includes Tiger Woods. Even Tiger waited until he was 21 to turn pro.

Michelle Wie was born in Honolulu, Hawaii, on October 11, 1989. Her parents, who are Korean, moved to the islands in 1988 after Michelle's dad got a job as a professor at the University of Hawaii. Bo, Michelle's mom, was an excellent golfer who introduced the game to B.J. after they met each other.

B.J. quickly became an excellent golfer, too, and the Wies joined a golf club in Hawaii. Not long after Michelle was born, she started following them around on the course. She was about four-and-a-half when she first started hitting a golf ball in 1994. By the time she was 7, Michelle already was shooting scores in the 80s for 18 holes. (Most grownups can't match that score on a regulation course!)

The Wies didn't push Michelle into golf—but they

Michelle swings hard during the 2003 Public **Links** event, one of the most important amateur golf tournaments in the U.S.

Young Michelle Wie

▶ Also was an excellent tennis player. But she decided she liked golf better because "you don't have to run!"

▶ Learned to speak several languages, including Korean and Japanese, in addition to English

▶ Once shot a 64 on a championship-length course when she was only 10 years old

▶ Was just 11 years old when she won Hawaii's state championship tournament for women

never held her back, either. She had an **obvious** love for the game and ability to play it. "We just never discouraged her," B.J. told *Fortune* magazine.

Michelle became so good at golf that the Wies eventually gave up the sport themselves to help her. In 2000, when Michelle was 10, she became the youngest person ever to qualify for the United States Amateur Public Links Championship. Two years later, at 12, she reached the semifinals of that event. She was the youngest player ever to reach that stage. And at 13 in 2003, she won the tournament. She was—you guessed it—the youngest winner ever!

CHAPTER 3

Breaking Ground with Every Shot

IN 1997, MICHELLE WIE WAS 7 YEARS OLD WHEN she watched Tiger Woods blow away the field by 12 strokes to win the Masters golf tournament in Augusta, Georgia. (The Masters is one of golf's most important events, one of the four major tournaments, or simply "majors," on the PGA Tour.) She decided then and there that she would one day play in the Masters, too. "I want to test my game at the highest level," Michelle says.

It never occurred to Michelle when she was watching on television that there were no girls playing in the Masters that afternoon. But once she found out, it didn't matter. "I still am going to win the Masters one day," she told herself.

If you're going to pick a role model, pick the best. Young Michelle studied every move of golfing great Tiger Woods.

Any golfer can enter the U.S. Public Links Championship. Winners of local events move on to state and then national finals. The event was first held in 1922.

As Michelle kept doing well, huge crowds followed her at every stop, including the 2004 Sony Open, held in her native Hawaii.

Just playing in the Masters would be a ground-breaking accomplishment. No woman has ever qualified for the field in the 70-plus-year history of the event. And the only way for Michelle to make it there as an amateur was to win the men's United States Amateur or the men's Amateur Public **Links** Championship.

Having already won the women's public links title in 2003, Michelle qualified to play in the men's tournament in 2005. It wasn't the first time she was the only woman in a field of male stars. In 2003, she played in tournaments on the Nationwide Tour (which is much like the minor leagues to the PGA Tour's major leagues) and the Canadian Tour, but missed the cut both times. In 2004 and 2005, she played in the PGA Tour's Sony Open in her native

Hawaii. She missed the cut both years there, too, but had a 2-under-par 68 in the second round in 2004 to post the lowest score ever by a woman in a PGA event.

At the 2005 United States Amateur Public Links Championship, Michelle won three matches, then lost in the round of eight to Clay Ogden, the eventual champion. "He played amazingly well," Michelle said **graciously** afterwards. "It wasn't like I was playing bad. He played really great."

Michelle's Masters dream was delayed, but not dead. "I'm the kind of person where if I really want something, I just have to do it," she said. Though no longer an amateur, she still hopes to find a way to Augusta, site of the Masters, via the PGA Tour. That might mean earning a Tour card through the annual Qualifying School, or it might mean entering selected PGA tournaments even while playing on the LPGA Tour.

"I still want to compete in some PGA events and to one day play in the Masters," she says. "That's my goal." If any young female golfer has a shot at that, it's Michelle.

Michelle's Big Moment

Michelle Wie stood on the tee of the par-5 14th hole of the U.S. Women's Amateur Public Links final in Long Grove, Illinois, in the summer of 2003. Michelle was tied with former college champion Virada Nirapathpongporn after 31 holes of the 36-hole final. But the 13-year-old Wie's tremendous length off the tee gave her an edge . . . and she was just about to take advantage. "Golf is a lot more fun when you take risks," Michelle explained later.

So she ripped a 313-yard drive into the fairway, then knocked her next shot onto the green. She made the putt for an eagle 3 that gave her the lead in the match. Michelle eventually went on to win 1-up and became the youngest titleist—man or woman—in more than 100 years of United States Golf Association adult championships. "This means a lot," Michelle said. "I never won a national championship before."

It may have been her first, but chances are that it won't be her last.

Michelle showed that she belonged with the pros with a second-place finish at the 2005 LPGA Championship.

CHAPTER 4

Turning Pro: Time to Earn

IN 2005, JUST SIX DAYS BEFORE SHE TURNED 16, Michelle Wie turned professional. From that point on, she was going to get paid to play golf. Until that point, though she played in pro events, she did not earn any money, no matter how high she finished.

Michelle certainly was not a newcomer to pro golf events. In addition to her appearances in the PGA Tour events, Michelle had played in 24 tournaments on the LPGA Tour—and she had made the cut in 16 of them. In the LPGA majors (the most important tournaments on the schedule), Michelle placed among the top 10 finishers four times in eight tries. Her best result was a second-place finish at the LPGA Championship in June of 2005.

Turning pro not only meant that Michelle could

keep her winnings from playing in professional golf tournaments, but it also meant she could get paid to endorse products for companies. Because of her talent, charm, and potential to attract both male and female fans of all ages, Michelle immediately signed big deals with Sony and with Nike. Those contracts, worth as much as $10 million according to some reports, made her the highest-paid female athlete in the world after tennis stars Maria Sharapova and Serena Williams—even though she had never won a professional tournament.

Michelle showed off her new partner by putting on the famous Nike "swoosh."

"I know I have to win," Michelle said at the press conference announcing her decision to turn pro. "That's my priority right now. Everyone expects me to do better and work hard, and I'm going to try my best."

With her fame, good looks, and unlimited future—plus endorsement money in the bank—things would seem to be perfect for a 16-year-old. Not everything has gone Michelle's way, though.

Michelle started her first full season as a pro golfer at the 2006 Sony Open, back home in Hawaii.

Other players, including both men and women, have occasionally been resentful of her endorsement contracts, **exemptions** into certain tournaments, and enormous media exposure at such a young age. As

Michelle's popularity extends worldwide. Here she meets a young fan (a future Michelle?) at an event in Japan.

the old saying goes, you can't please everyone. Most people associated with the PGA and LPGA Tours, however, appreciate what Michelle brings to the game.

"Michelle is good for golf, just as Tiger Woods

What is an exemption? Tournament organizers can award entry to golfers who have not otherwise earned it. Sometimes these are local golfers. Michelle got exemptions for her ability to attract fans.

Going for the Green

Michelle Wie played in seven LPGA tour events in 2005. She was an amateur, then, so she could not collect any money for the tournaments. But if you add up all the money she would have won, it amounts to more than $640,000!

is good for golf," LPGA Tour commissioner Carolyn Bivens said. "There are a lot of people who may not follow golf otherwise, but tune in when you've got Michelle or Tiger out there."

Those people were watching when Michelle made her professional debut at the 2005 Samsung World Championships in Palm Desert, California. It was a memorable debut—but for all the wrong reasons. After apparently finishing in fourth place, Michelle was disqualified for an incorrect drop during the third round. (When a player hits a ball into a place from which they can't hit it again, they are given a chance to drop the ball in a safe place.)

The mistake cost Michelle more than $53,000 (the fourth-place check she had to give up when she was disqualified). That's a lot of money by any standards—even for a big-money athlete like Michelle—and Michelle was understandably disappointed. But there was a silver lining. She won over a lot of fans that day with her mature

After finding her ball, Michelle dropped it into a new place—only to find out later it was an illegal place to drop.

reaction to the controversy. "I'm really sad that this happened," she told reporters afterward. "But the rules are the rules. I respect that."

On and off the course, Michelle has earned a great deal of respect herself at a young age.

Long off the tee and pretty darned smart off the course, Michelle Wie can look ahead to a bright future in golf.

Michelle Wie Time Line

1989 Born in Honolulu, Hawaii

1994 Begins playing golf

2000 Shoots a 64 for 18 holes at the age of 10

2000 Qualifies for the U.S. Women's Public Links Championship for the first time

2002 Plays in her first LPGA event (the Takefuji Classic)

2003 Becomes the youngest winner of the U.S. Women's Public Links Championship

2004 At 15, is the youngest golfer to play in a PGA Tour event (the Sony Open)

2005 Turns professional and signs major endorsement deals with Sony and Nike

2006 For the first time, qualifies for weekend play ("makes the cut") in a men's tournament, the SK Telecom Open in South Korea

GLOSSARY

amateur   a person who is not paid to take part in an activity, in this case golf

birdie   a golf term meaning a score of one below par on a single hole

exemption   an exception to rules made so that someone who would not normally take part can do so

extraordinary   surprisingly good and well above normal

graciously   kindly, politely

links   another word for a golf course; it comes from the way courses were first laid out, as a linked series of fairways along a coastline.

obvious   very clear to any observer

BOOKS

Michelle Wie
By Geoffrey M. Horn
(Gareth Stevens Publishing, Milwaukee) 2005
This book for younger readers follows Wie from her childhood to her current status as one of the world's most recognizable female athletes.

Michelle Wie: The Making of a Champion
By Jennifer Mario
(St. Martin's, New York) 2006
This book covers Wie's amazing career in words and pictures. It includes photos and interviews with family, friends and competitors.

Michelle Wie: She's Got the Power!
By Cynthia A. Dean
(Edge Books, Minnesota) 2005
This book celebrates Wie's talents and focuses on her competitive spirit.

WEB SITES

Visit our home page for lots of links about Michelle Wie:
www.childsworld.com/links

Note to Parents, Teachers, and Librarians: We routinely check our Web links to make sure they're safe, active sites—so encourage your readers to check them out!

INDEX

ABOUT THE AUTHOR

Jim Gigliotti is a writer who lives in southern California with his wife and two children. A former editor with the National Football League's publishing division, he has written more than a dozen books about sports and personalities, including *Stadium Stories: USC Trojans* and *Watching Football* (with former NFL star Daryl Johnston).